A Daily Dose of Dad Jokes

A
DAILY DOSE
OF DAD JOKES

365 TRULY TERRIBLE WISECRACKS
(YOU'VE BEEN WARNED)

TAYLOR CALMUS AND PETER L. HARMON

ROCKRIDGE
PRESS

Interior and Cover Designer: Eric Pratt
Art Producer: Sue Bischofberger
Editor: Erin Nelson
Production Manager: Riley Hoffman
Production Editors: Melissa Edeburn and Erum Khan

Illustrations © 2019 Dylan Goldberger
Author photos © Morgan Ayres

ISBN: Print 978-1-64152-655-5 | eBook 978-1-64152-656-2

THIS BOOK IS DEDICATED
TO OUR DADS, WHO INSPIRED
OUR LOVE OF DAD JOKES,
OUR WIVES, WHO PUT UP WITH
OUR DAD JOKES, AND, OF COURSE,
OUR KIDS, WHO PRETEND TO LAUGH
AT EACH JOKE WE MAKE.

Taylor

Hey there!

Pete

Taylor and Pete here. We're a couple of dads who love a good (or so bad it's good) dad joke. We like to think of ourselves as the Oprahs of dad jokes: "You get a dad joke; you get a dad joke. Look underneath your seat—yep, there's a dad joke under there!" To which you would respond, "Under where?"and we would cackle because we made you say *underwear*.

But what is a dad joke?

A dad joke can be many things: a pun, a quip, a made-up story, a one-liner, a two-liner, an ocean liner. As long as it takes you on a ride and the punchline gives you one of those smiles that you don't want to let cross your face—that's a dad joke.

It's our belief that dad jokes aren't just for dads. They're for us all. And even though they might elicit some coworker or spousal side-eye, what they are also sure to do is surprise and delight the most cherished people in your life. That's what we hope this collection does for you.

So, get your grins and groans ready, and thank the person who gave you this honorary entrance into the Dad Joke Hall of Fame. Welcome to *A Daily Dose of Dad Jokes*.

JANUARY

Went to Disneyland because my daughter's obsessed with Mickey Mouse. She was so excited when I got home and told her. — Ryan Reynolds

1
JANUARY

**Did you hear about the dad who
burned the Hawaiian pizza?**

He should have put it on aloha temperature.

2
JANUARY

Bowling jokes are right up my alley.

2

JANUARY

Why did the couple buy stale bread on their wedding day?

They wanted to grow mold together.

JANUARY

I went to a comedy club the other night and a pig was performing. Honestly, he was a total boar.

5

JANUARY

How did the carpenter find her spouse?
She used a stud finder.

6

JANUARY

If you want a job in the lotion industry, the best
advice I can give you is to apply daily.

7

JANUARY

I got you a refrigerator for your birthday. I can't
wait to see your face light up when you open it.

8

JANUARY

What goes tick tock, woof woof?

A watchdog.

9

JANUARY

Whenever I travel, I take the late-night flight because there's no extra charge for checking the bags under my eyes.

JANUARY

Do you want to hear a pizza joke?

Never mind, it's too cheesy.

**Did you hear about the crust that
ate too much cheese?**

It was stuffed.

Did you hear about the supreme pizza? No?

Okay, olive you alone and stop peppering you
with pizza jokes.

JANUARY

What has four tires and flies?

A garbage truck.

JANUARY

Three brothers were going on a trek through the desert. One brother said, "I'm going to bring water, so that if we get thirsty, we have something to drink." Another brother said, "I'm going to bring food, so that if we get hungry, we have something to eat." The third brother, known for his inventiveness, said, "I'm going to bring a car door." The other two brothers looked at him and asked, "Why?" He smiled and said, "If it gets too hot, we can roll down the window."

JANUARY

Did you hear about the fish with the bad report card?

All his grades were under "C."

JANUARY

Dad: Doctor, I think I have five legs.
Doctor: How do your pants fit?
Dad: Like a glove.

JANUARY

SPOILER ALERT: Milk goes bad in 15 days.

JANUARY

I saw a job listing for a web producer. Turns out they were just looking for a spider.

JANUARY

A young ribbon took her piece-of-string boyfriend home. Her father, a military ribbon, took one look at the string and declared: "Absolutely not. There is no way my daughter is dating a common piece of string." The piece of string ran out of the house, very out of sorts, working himself into a frenzy. When he finally marched back into the house, the father said, "What are you doing here? You're a real piece of string, aren't you?" The string replied, "No, sir. I'm a frayed knot."

18
JANUARY

People don't like to have to bend down for their drinks. We really need to raise the bar.

19
JANUARY

A pencil was fidgeting in class. The teacher said, "What's the matter? Do you have to use the restroom?" "Yes," said the pencil, "number two!"

JANUARY

Had a weird dream last night that I was a muffler. I woke up exhausted.

JANUARY

There was a group of scallywags who traversed the globe on a ship, pirated other boats, and loved to go rock climbing. This nefarious clan of rogues waged war on the ocean blue, searched for buried treasure, and practiced tying knots. I'm telling you, they loved two things: finding bounty and scaling walls. They were the Pirates of the Carabiner.

22
JANUARY

Did you hear about that movie on abdominal workouts?

It was a total belly flop.

23
JANUARY

When I was a teenager, I got my first computer. That led me down a road of buying more and more computers. In fact, I was hooked on computers. I'll tell you though, sometimes I miss that first Gateway computer.

24

JANUARY

Why can't you hear it when a pterodactyl goes to the bathroom?

Because the "P" is silent!

25

JANUARY

I just got the world's worst thesaurus. Not only is it terrible, it's also terrible … and terrible.

JANUARY

What does a pepper do when it's angry?

It gets jalapeño (hal-ah-pen-yo) face.

JANUARY

This graveyard looks crowded.
People must be dying to get in here.

28

A heel, an elbow, and a toe walk into a bar. They have a few drinks and then the heel says, "That's enough for me. I'll call a taxi." Eventually, the elbow heads home, too. The toe keeps drinking until finally the bartender says, "Hey, do you need a ride?" The toe responds, "Don't worry about me. I'll take a toe truck."

JANUARY

Did you know gophers throw super hip, exclusive parties?

They're just really hard to get into because they're underground.

JANUARY

I downloaded an app on my phone that makes the phone combust if somebody takes a picture of themselves. It's called the Selfie Destruct Button.

JANUARY

Why couldn't the lifeguard save the hippie?

The hippie was too far out, man.

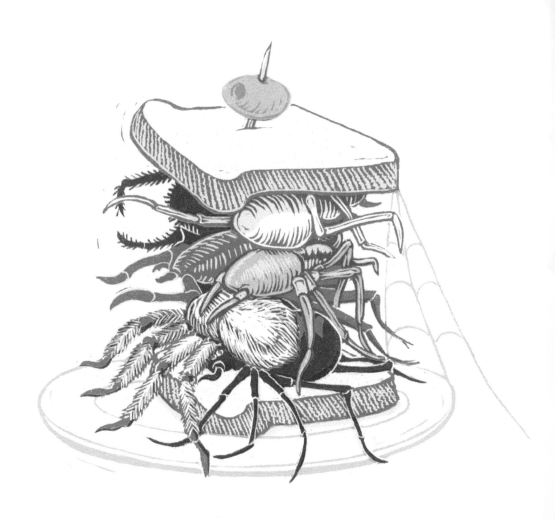

FEBRUARY

My current alarm clock is the blood-curdling screams that I wake up to. I bolt down the hallway thinking that someone's fallen out of their crib or broken their arm or, I don't know, drowning in the sink, and then they're just like "Good morning, Mommy!" — *Kristen Bell*

1

FEBRUARY

Did you hear about the math student who's afraid of negative numbers?

He'll stop at nothing to avoid them.

2

FEBRUARY

Dad: Do you want to hear a
Groundhog Day joke?
Son: Yes.

Dad: Do you want to hear a
Groundhog Day joke?
Son: Yes.

Dad: Do you want to hear a
Groundhog Day joke?
Son: I said, "Yes!!"

FEBRUARY

What do you call it when a crab replaces a batter?

A pinch hitter.

FEBRUARY

I told my actor friend to "break a leg" because he said he was trying to get cast.

FEBRUARY

I bought a dictionary and when I got it home, I found out that all the pages were blank. I have no words to describe how angry I am.

FEBRUARY

What's more useful than the invention of the first telephone?

The second one.

FEBRUARY

Why did the guy try to eat his e-mail?
All that spam.

FEBRUARY

Scientists say humans swallow eight spiders
per year, so I like to get all of mine out of the
way at once.

FEBRUARY

When I was in high school, my mom made me keep a box of candy in my car. She said it could be a real lifesaver.

FEBRUARY

Why did the server bring the customer an iPhone charger?

He asked for apple juice.

FEBRUARY

I used to have this dog named Rex. Every day, I'd put his leash on and take him for a walk. Then he died, and now he's kind of a drag.

FEBRUARY

Dad: Did you hear about the new movie on constipation?

Son: No.

Dad: That's because it never came out.

FEBRUARY

I used to date this girl named Ruth. She made me happy, and when I was with her, I was always a better person. Then she dumped me. Now, I'm ruthless.

FEBRUARY

Two pickles were in love. One turned to the other and said, "You mean a great dill to me."

FEBRUARY

Why was the superhero the one to flush the toilet?

It was his duty.

FEBRUARY

Let's take a minute to remember the boiled water. It will be mist.

FEBRUARY

When I was visiting the White House, I noticed a framed puzzle hanging in the Oval Office. While I was admiring it, the president approached and said, "Fantastic, really, really terrific. They said it couldn't be done, but I did it. I do the best puzzles, everyone says so, and this one, the box said three to five years, but it only took me one month."

FEBRUARY

What's the easiest way to remember your wife's birthday?

Forget it once.

FEBRUARY

The kids couldn't see the new pirate movie because it was rated "Arrrgh!"

FEBRUARY

I've always struggled to eat Cobb salads. A couple of weeks ago, my stomach started giving me trouble, so I went to the doctor. He checked me out and said he had some troubling news. "What?" I asked. "Well," the doctor said, "there's a piece of lettuce sticking out of your rear." "Okay," I said, "is that bad?" The doctor frowned and said, "That's just the tip of the iceberg."

FEBRUARY

Don't ever serve lobster at your benefit.
They're really so shellfish.

FEBRUARY

Why did the grape buy guitars for all his friends?
He wanted to jam.

FEBRUARY

My e-mail password was hacked again. That's
the fifth time I've had to rename my dog.

24
FEBRUARY

The Surgeon General says listening to too much Queen can be hazardous to your health. It's probably because of the high Mercury content.

25
FEBRUARY

If Disney made a movie about Mardi Gras, it would be called Beauty and the Beads.

FEBRUARY

A guy went to see his therapist, who noticed the man's mood was lighter. The therapist asked, "Has anything changed in your life?" "Yeah," the guy said, "I got fired from my job." "You got fired?" asked the therapist. "Why do you seem so happy?" "Well," said the guy, "I worked at a can-crushing factory. It was soda pressing."

FEBRUARY

I got an e-mail from Costco and it looks like they do mortgages now. The only problem is you need to buy about 30 houses.

FEBRUARY

Did you hear about the origami teacher who quit?

Too much paperwork.

MARCH

Electricity can be dangerous. My nephew tried to stick a penny into a plug. Whoever said a penny doesn't go far didn't see him shoot across that floor. — Tim Allen

1
MARCH

Kid: Dad, are we pyromaniacs?

Dad: Yes, we arson.

2
MARCH

My wife asked me to do some odd jobs.
She gave me a list of 10, so I did one, three,
five, seven, and nine.

MARCH

I'm on a nuts and berries diet. My kids
drive me nuts, then I bury my
emotions with food.

MARCH

A son noticed that his father's mail had ended up
all over the yard and stuck to the exterior walls.
When confronted by his son, the dad said, "You young
people have no appreciation for snail mail."

5

MARCH

I really used to like my psychic, until I threw her a surprise party and it worked.

6

MARCH

What do you call a sleeping bull?

A bulldozer.

MARCH

I'm always on the edge of my seat when I'm at the circus. It's just so in tents.

MARCH

Who is the coolest doctor at the hospital?

The hip doctor.

9

MARCH

I haven't owned a watch for I don't know how long.

10

MARCH

Why did Spider-Man go to the doctor?

His spidey sense was tingling.

MARCH

A balloon was becoming a famous musical artist. She started her career at birthday parties, then began getting booked everywhere. One day, a big producer called her and asked her to sign an amazing record deal. She said, "I'm sorry, but I can't." "Why?" asked the music producer. "Well," the balloon said, "I'm afraid of going pop."

12

MARCH

Did you hear the joke about the time the mosquito landed on my leg?

It was a knee slapper.

13

MARCH

Why couldn't the vampire's wife sleep?

Because of his coffin.

MARCH

Why does the astronaut spend late nights on the computer?

He's a fan of the space bar.

MARCH

Did you hear about the dad who couldn't drive his kids and their friends underground?

He had carpool tunnel syndrome.

16

MARCH

Which country's capital has the fastest-growing population?

Ireland. Every day it's Dublin.

17

MARCH

Who stays out all night on St. Patrick's Day?

Paddy O'Furniture.

MARCH

A tortoise got into an accident. It was a
turtle disaster.

MARCH

My coworker brought toast to the copy room
because he heard the printer was jammed.

20
MARCH

I'm so excited for spring that I might
wet my plants.

21
MARCH

A judge went to the dentist and was feeling very
nervous. When the dentist walked in, the judge
demanded an oath: "Do you swear to pull the tooth, the
whole tooth, and nothing but the tooth?"

22

MARCH

What did the time traveler do when she was still hungry after her meal?

She went back four seconds.

23

MARCH

Dad: I don't trust trees.
Son: Why not?
Dad: There's something shady about them.

24
MARCH

Where might you get a haircut and hot dog?
A barber-Q.

25
MARCH

Want to hear a dirty joke?
A dog jumped into a mud puddle.

Want to hear a clean joke?
A dog jumped into a bath.

26

MARCH

//////////////////////////

Knock! Knock!
Who's there?
Norma Lee.
Norma Lee who?
**Norma Lee I have my key.
Can you let me in?**

27

MARCH

//////////////////////////

I love to start my mornings on the beach.
I say hello to the ocean, and it waves back.

28

MARCH

When I was in college, I used to be a pickpocket.
I once stole a watch right off Dwayne Johnson, but
he saw me. I took off running and he chased me down
an alley. Unfortunately, it was a brick wall dead end.
I turned around to see Dwayne closing in, and that
was it: I was between The Rock and a hard place.

29

MARCH

I don't know how to make a good cup of tea,
but I'm chai-ing my best.

30
MARCH

A dad was washing his car with his son until the son said, "Dad, can you please just use a sponge?"

31
MARCH

What do you call a pony with a sore throat?

A little horse.

APRIL

Why are gas stations so excited on April 1?

It's April Fuels' Day!

APRIL

Why is everyone so tired at the beginning of April?

Because they just finished a 31-day March.

APRIL

My boss kicked me out of our weekly group meetings because I was making thunder noises every few minutes. I guess he doesn't appreciate how I brainstorm.

APRIL

Did you hear about the almond who ate vegetables, ran every morning, and took vitamins?

He was a total health nut.

APRIL

I always found it a little counterproductive
when a teacher would say,
"Don't get smart with me."

APRIL

What did one plate say to the other?

"Dinner is on me."

APRIL

///////////////

My wife started a business where she sells candles that don't smell like anything. The customer reaction has been poor. The candles don't make scents, so my wife doesn't make cents. Does that make sense?

APRIL

Why did the owner fire all the Williams in his office?

He was tired of paying his Bills.

APRIL

My daughter dropped an ice cube in the kitchen. She was pretty worried about it, but I said, "Don't worry, honey. In a few minutes it will be water under the fridge."

APRIL

A cat sits in jail with a camera phone. What's she doing?

Taking cell-fleas.

APRIL

Everyone has a favorite word. Mine is "drool." It just rolls off the tongue.

12
APRIL

Knock! Knock!
Who's there?
Pencil.
Pencil who?
Pencil fall down if you don't wear a belt.

13
APRIL

My Gram always supports my photography. Whenever I need something, boom, she's right there. I love my Instagram.

14
APRIL

What do you call a pile of kittens?

A meowntain.

APRIL

I thought it would be cool to have Velcro® shoes, but it turns out they're a total rip-off.

16
APRIL

What was the nacho's favorite dance?
Salsa.

What about the soda?
Can-can.

The rabbit's?
Hip hop.

The tree's?
Swing.

The robot vacuum's?
Rumba.

What was the eyeball's least favorite dance?
The polka.

APRIL

I don't like to talk about my pan pizza.
It's personal.

APRIL

Why do monkeys' marriages never last?

They're all swingers.

APRIL

My hipster girlfriend likes to take pictures of her coffee. She calls them mugshots.

APRIL

Did you hear about the hotel room with a living room and a kitchen?

It's pretty suite.

APRIL

My wife came to me quite stressed. "Honey, I'm worried about our daughter," she said. "She's playing with sticks, pretending they're going on a date and falling in love, but then she lights their heads on fire." "It's okay," I told her. "She's just a matchmaker."

APRIL

The bank sent me a new credit card, claiming it had chip technology, but when I dunked it in French Onion Dip, it still tasted like plastic.

APRIL

BOILER ALERT: If you heat water on a stove for several minutes, it will bubble.

24

APRIL

What did the left eye say to the right eye?

"Between you and me, something smells."

25

APRIL

They should do another Harry Potter movie
when Harry retires. They could call it
Harry Potter and the Kidney Stones.

APRIL

My dad and I snuck up on several hundred rabbits all munching on grass in a field. Then all of a sudden one of them spotted me, and in a flash the rabbits all jumped into a single file line and hopped away. My dad yelled, "Now that's what I call a receding hare line!"

27
APRIL

Why was that dog arrested?

He was living the pug life.

28
APRIL

My son resisted puberty at first, but it's starting to grow on him.

29

APRIL

What kind of cheese surrounds a castle?

Moatzarella.

30

APRIL

What do you call an elephant that doesn't matter?

Irrelephant.

MAY

Two kids are easier than one because they play together. When you have one, you have to be the show. When you've got two, you're just an usher. — Chris Rock

1
MAY

I crashed my bread truck and it started a fire.
Now it's toast.

2
MAY

What do you call a deer with no eyes?
No eye deer.

MAY

One scientist pointed to a cloning machine and said, "I don't understand how this thing works." The other scientist said, "That makes two of us."

MAY

A farmer told me that he had a hen who would count her eggs every day. She was a mathemachicken.

MAY

I drank a bottle of food coloring yesterday.
I dyed a little inside.

MAY

Why don't ants get sick?

They have all the right antibodies.

MAY

When is a door not a door?

When it's ajar.

MAY

Always borrow money from a pessimist.
They won't expect it back.

MAY

Every year Godzilla looks forward to Mothra's Day.

MAY

What do you call someone who pretends to be Swedish?

An artificial Swedener.

MAY

I helped my dad install a new window in his living room. It was such a pane.

MAY

The fact that our planet fully rotates in 24 hours really makes my day.

MAY

There was a study that proved fast food chicken is only 50 percent chicken, which is not great if you want a chicken sandwich. But it is great if you're trying to quit chicken.

MAY

Why are there so many pizza places in Chicago?

They're all trying to get a piece of the pie.

MAApply

MAY

I once saw a man at the beach yelling, "Help, shark!," which to me is so strange. If I needed help, a shark would be the last thing I'd call for.

MAY

A high-ranking officer approached a young soldier. The officer got right in the young soldier's face and said, "Soldier, I didn't see you at camouflage training this morning." The young soldier suppressed a smile and said, "Thank you, sir!"

17

MAY

What do you call a can opener that doesn't work?

A can't opener.

18

MAY

Want to hear a joke about paper?

Never mind, it's tearable.

Did you hear the one about the sheep?

It's baaaad.

What about the joke about the bread?

It's pretty crumby.

19
MAY

Knock! Knock!
Who's there?
Chicken.
Chicken who?
**Chicken your pockets if you
can't find your wallet.**

20
MAY

**What is the Nevada city that dentists
love to visit most?**
Floss Vegas.

21
MAY

///////////////

How does Mom always know what the weather will be?

She has a your-mom-meter.

22
MAY

///////////////

Two antennas got married on a roof. Everyone said the ceremony wasn't anything special, but the reception was fantastic.

23
MAY

\/\/\/\/\/\/\/\/

Why did the camera get sick from its meal?

Too much raw footage.

24
MAY

\/\/\/\/\/\/\/\/

A jumper cable walked into a cafe. The barista looked at the cable, rolled his eyes, and said, "You again?" The jumper cable shrugged. The barista said, "Okay, I'll get you a coffee, just try not to start anything."

25
MAY

I debated showing up to a pool party with six-pack abs or without working out at all. After a lot of consideration, I decided to go with my gut.

26
MAY

I love chalkboards. They're remarkable.

MAY

I knew this couple who met on a carousel.
I think they're still going 'round together.

MAY

Dad: Be careful out there—it's
raining cats and dogs.

Son: Okay, Dad.

Dad: Seriously, it's dangerous.
You could step in a poodle.

29

MAY

The past, present, and future walked into a bar together. It was tense.

30

MAY

Where did the general keep his armies?

In his sleevies.

31

MAY

What do you call two buddies who wear jackets with no sleeves?

Vest friends.

JUNE

Be nice to your children, for they will choose your nursing home.
— attributed to Phyllis Diller

JUNE

I can't remember how boomerangs work.
Hopefully, it will come back to me.

JUNE

**Did you hear about the computer that
showed up late for work?**

It had a hard drive.

JUNE

Installing mirrors is a job I could really see myself doing.

JUNE

Why did Humpty Dumpty have a great fall?

To make up for his miserable summer.

5

JUNE

A guy went to the blood bank to donate blood.
He asked the phlebotomist what type of blood
he had. "Type A," the phlebotomist said. "Hmm,"
said the guy, "on my medical record it said 'Type B.'"
The phlebotomist replied, "I see. Well, that must
have been a Type O."

6

JUNE

**My wife texted me and told me to call her back.
I wonder what Back wants?**

JUNE

What do you call a belt made of watches?

A waist of time.

JUNE

When I work in the garden, it strains my eyes.
I should really get some weeding glasses.

JUNE

Did you hear about the two guys who stole a calendar?

They each got six months.

JUNE

How many tickles does it take to make an octopus laugh?

Ten tickles.

11

JUNE

////////////////

I paid for a ceiling fan the other day, but it was a total waste of money. He just stands there cheering.

12

JUNE

////////////////

A bunch of novelists in my neighborhood hit a rough spot, so we had a writer's block party.

JUNE

What's the difference between a fancy man
on a bicycle and a casual man on a tricycle?

A tire.

JUNE

I don't like to toot my own horn. And that's why
my trumpet business is struggling.

15

JUNE

What did the digital clock say to its mom?

"Look, Ma, no hands!"

16

JUNE

The waiter keeps asking me if I wanna box for my leftovers, but I'd rather wrestle him for them.

17

JUNE

Why did the duck overheat?

Because he was a firequacker.

18

JUNE

I love telling dad jokes. Sometimes he laughs.

JUNE

Did you hear about the book on the history of scratch-and-sniff stickers?

It was a best smeller and it made a lot of scents. Odor it today.

JUNE

With kids, you spend the first two years teaching them how to walk and talk, then you spend the next 16 years telling them to keep quiet and sit down.

JUNE

Knock! Knock!

Who's there?

A dad.

A dad who?

A dad who loves you.

Aww, Happy Father's Day, Dad.

Thanks. Now open the door. I lost my keys.

JUNE

Did you know the first French fries weren't actually cooked in France?

They were cooked in Greece.

JUNE

How do trees access the Internet?

They log in.

JUNE

What do you call miniature cattle?

Portabull.

JUNE

My dog likes to trick me when we're playing fetch. Whenever he's about to give me back the stick, he takes off running again. The vet warned me he's a Labrador Deceiver.

JUNE

My doctor says I don't need to worry about the bird flu because it's tweetable.

27

JUNE

Maybe it's time we started telling hot chocolate
she is also smart chocolate.

28

JUNE

Why are cheetahs terrible at hide-and-seek?

They're always spotted.

JUNE

Why is the scarecrow's confidence so high?

He's constantly outstanding in his field.

JUNE

How often should you tell jokes about the elements?

Periodically.

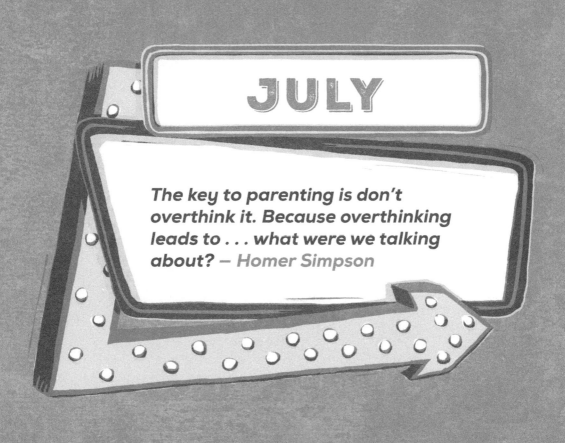

JULY

The key to parenting is don't overthink it. Because overthinking leads to . . . what were we talking about? — *Homer Simpson*

1
JULY

Want to hear a joke about construction?
Never mind, I'm still working on it.

2
JULY

Taking his son to school, the dad began reversing the car down the driveway. The dad got a wistful look in his eye and stopped the car. "What's wrong?" asked his son. "Nothing," said the dad, then put the car in reverse again. "This just takes me back."

3
JULY

What did E.T.'s dad say when he finally returned home?

"Where on Earth have you been?"

4
JULY

Why are there no knock-knock jokes about democracy?

Because freedom rings.

5

JULY

A guy without any experience applied for a job at a restaurant. The manager asked skeptically, "Why would you be good at this job?" The guy thought about it and said, "Well, I could bring a lot to the table."

6

JULY

I'm worried about the math teacher holding graph paper. She's definitely plotting something.

/////////////////

Where do you learn to make ice cream?

Sundae School.

/////////////////

Did you hear about the steps everyone couldn't stop looking at?

It was a flight of stares.

JULY

What do you call a shoe made out of a banana?

A slipper.

JULY

What did the fisherman say to the magician?

"Pick a cod, any cod."

A dairy farmer made sure his cows were treated well. He let them roam on an enormous field where they grazed nonstop. He made sure that the cows were cool enough in the summer and warm enough in the winter. He even began singing to them at night. Once in a while, he would sneak out to the pasture and give his cows massages. The farmer's wife had had enough. One night, when the farmer crept back into the house, she confronted him. "You need to stop treating those cows so well," she said. "Why?" asked the farmer. "Well," his wife said, "if you keep pampering those cows, you're going to get spoiled milk."

JULY

//////////////

How many apples grow on a tree?

All of them.

JULY

//////////////

What did the modest stoplight say to the car?

"Don't look, I'm changing."

JULY

What is Forrest Gump's computer password?

1Forrest1.

JULY

Two parents saw that their child was covered in bumps so they rushed her to the doctor. The doctor examined the child and said there were a couple of ways to treat the ailment. "Whoa, whoa, whoa," the dad said, shaking his head. "Let's not make any rash decisions!"

JULY

Why don't you ever want to run in front of a car?
You'll get tired.

Why don't you ever want to run behind a car?
You'll get exhausted.

JULY

I could never figure out how to fasten my
seatbelt, but then it clicked.

JULY

Once when walking down the street, a man found a locket with a picture of a charming lady inside. He devoted his life to finding this woman, searching for years and years. When his friends asked him how he stayed hopeful, the man said, "I just really admire in-de-pendant women."

19
JULY

Why wasn't the sweet potato allowed in the band?
They wanted to have a yam session.

20
JULY

I can never make reservations at the library.
They're always completely booked.

JULY 21

//////////////

My wife enjoys it when I blow air on her when she's hot, but honestly, I'm not a fan.

JULY 22

//////////////

Did you hear Old MacDonald's son joined the army?

They call him "E.I. G.I. Joe."

23
JULY

///////////////

Dad: I don't like "oyings."
Kid: What's an "oying"?
Dad: This joke!

24
JULY

///////////////

Yesterday, a potted plant fell on my head.
I only have my shelf to blame.

JULY

Did you hear about the headphones that became friends?

They were earbuds.

JULY

Did you hear about the guy who was addicted to brake fluid?

The good news is he could stop at any time.

JULY

Knock! Knock!
Who's there?
Broken pencil.
Broken pencil who?
Never mind, it's pointless.

28

JULY

What's Beethoven's favorite fruit?

Ba-na-na-naaaa. Ba-na-na-naaaa.

29
JULY

I don't trust stairs. They're always so up and down.

30
JULY

Why do ducks have feathers?

To cover their butt quacks.

31

JULY

A carton of milk and a bottle of ketchup were hanging out in the refrigerator.

"Hey," the milk said to the ketchup, "did you hear the rumor about the butter?"

The ketchup was intrigued. "No! What happened?"

The milk thought twice. "Well, if you haven't heard, maybe I shouldn't tell you."

"Why not?" asked the ketchup. "I promise not to spread it!"

AUGUST

When your children are teenagers, it's important to have a dog so that someone In the house is happy to see you. — *Nora Ephron*

1

What did the drummer name his two daughters?

Anna One, Anna Two.

2

If your house doesn't have numbers on it, that's something you need to address.

AUGUST

I just burned 2,000 calories. It was easy. I just
fell asleep with a batch of cookies in the oven.

AUGUST

My dad thinks he's an optimist. He always says,
"Cheer up, son, it could be worse. You could
be stuck underground in a hole full of water."
I know he means well.

AUGUST

Did you hear about the celebrity who accidentally glued himself to his autobiography?

That's his story and he's sticking to it.

AUGUST

A pirate went to see a surgeon and said he wanted his spine removed. The surgeon asked him why he would ever want to have his spine removed. "Arrrgh," said the pirate, "it's holding me back!"

AUGUST

You never see hippos hiding in trees.
They must be really good at it.

AUGUST

**Did you hear about the optometrist
who loved jokes?**

The cornea the better.

AUGUST

What did the mom spider say to her teen?

"You spend too much time on the web."

AUGUST

How can you make the water bed bouncier?

Use spring water.

AUGUST

A husband remodels the bathroom and finds his wife doesn't like it. He says to her, "Honey, we just need to let it sink in."

AUGUST

My favorite time on a clock is 6:30.
Hands down.

AUGUST

What do you call a guy with a rubber toe?

Roberto.

AUGUST

Why do bears have hairy coats?

Fur protection.

AUGUST

**What word starts with "E," ends with "E,"
and only has one letter in it?**

Envelope.

AUGUST

The other day I was making a sandwich and had just
sliced a tomato in half when my daughter walked in
and said, "No! What are you doing? I wanted
whole tomatoes!" "Don't worry," I said. "We
have tomato paste."

AUGUST

Do you know how heavy the sun is?

Me neither, but it seems pretty light.

AUGUST

I just found out I'm colorblind. The diagnosis came totally out of the purple.

AUGUST

My friend told me he's quitting his job to become a mime. I haven't heard from him since.

A friend asked his perpetual bachelor friend, "Why aren't you married?" The man replied, "Well, I've dated a lot of people, but when I brought them home, my mother didn't like them." His friend thought for a moment and said, "I've got the perfect solution: Date someone who's just like your mother." A few months later they met again, and the man's friend asked, "Did you find the right one?" The man frowned. "Yes, I found the perfect person—just like my mother—and my mother was very happy." The friend said, "Then what's the problem?" The man replied, "My father didn't like her."

AUGUST

What rock group has four guys who don't sing?

Mount Rushmore.

AUGUST

I haven't bought a burial plot yet. Honestly, it's the last thing I need.

AUGUST

My brother used to be addicted to the Hokey Pokey, but thankfully he got treatment and turned himself around.

AUGUST

Have you seen my box of vintage candy canes?

They're in mint condition.

AUGUST

How do you stop a charging bull?

You take away its credit card.

AUGUST

My best friend is like my hairline.
We go way back.

AUGUST

We've got a problem with the roof, but it's okay.
I'm on top of it.

AUGUST

How did the Romans cut their hair?

With a pair of Caesars.

AUGUST

For our anniversary, I ordered my wife a reversible jacket. I can't wait to see how it turns out.

AUGUST

While we were on vacation in the mountains, Dad said, "Man, that's a big rock!" I said, "Boulder." Dad stuck out his chest and shouted, "MAN, THAT'S A BIG ROCK!"

AUGUST

When I die, I want to go peacefully in my sleep like my grandfather did, not screaming and yelling like the guy in his passenger seat.

SEPTEMBER

I pride myself on being a good dad, but my daughter learned to walk in a mall. What can I say, I like a food court.
— Tony Hale

1
SEPTEMBER

Did you hear that the Hulk started recycling?
He's really going green.

2
SEPTEMBER

The moon works really hard.
It pulls all-nighters almost every night.

SEPTEMBER

Me: Dad, I'm hungry.

Dad: Hi, Hungry. I'm Dad.

SEPTEMBER

What's the difference between the United States and a flash drive?

USA and USB.

SEPTEMBER

What's sad and doesn't weigh very much?
Light blue.

SEPTEMBER

A construction worker handed a steamroller driver a wad of cash, which the steamroller driver didn't even count. Another construction worker asked the first construction worker, "How'd you know how much to pay him?" The worker replied, "Oh, it's easy—he charges a flat fee."

SEPTEMBER

What do you call an exploding monkey?

A ba-boom.

SEPTEMBER

Whenever my best friends and I play hide-and-seek, it goes on for hours. Good friends are so hard to find.

SEPTEMBER

Did you hear about the sausage convention?

It was the Wurst.

SEPTEMBER

Some nights, I lie awake thinking about how our oceans are full of millions of jellyfish and not a single peanut butter fish.

SEPTEMBER

Do you want to hear a joke about dogs?

Never mind, it's a little far-fetched.

SEPTEMBER

What's the distance from the curb to the front door of a suburban house?

One yard.

SEPTEMBER

Picking your nose on an elevator is wrong on so many levels.

SEPTEMBER

Did you know there was no place to wash your hands on the Titanic?

It was deemed unsinkable.

SEPTEMBER

I used to be against being an organ donor.
Then I had a change of heart.

SEPTEMBER

**When a mom ladder with a kid marries another
ladder, what does that ladder become?**

A stepladder.

SEPTEMBER

A prisoner escapes from prison. He tunnels underground for miles until he pops up in a random backyard where a kid is playing. The prisoner is so excited to be out of prison and see the sunlight. "I'm free! I'm free!" he yells. The child looks at him, unimpressed. "So what?" the kid says. "I'm four."

SEPTEMBER

A canopy is the most snarky yard accessory. It's always throwing shade.

SEPTEMBER

Bro, do you want this pamphlet?

Yeah, brochure.

SEPTEMBER

Giraffes can grow up to 15 feet,
but most only have four.

SEPTEMBER

Have you ever played golf on a submarine?

It's subpar.

22

SEPTEMBER

What did the tree say to its branches in autumn?

"Leaf me alone."

23

SEPTEMBER

I love having movie marathons with my dog.
He never lets me miss anything if I have to
get up. I just say, "Hey, paws it."

24

SEPTEMBER

What do you call a nose with no body?

Nobody Nose.

SEPTEMBER

You should have seen their wedding. It was so beautiful, even the cake was in tiers.

SEPTEMBER

I just took my final exam to graduate from culinary school. It was a piece of cake.

27

SEPTEMBER

A guy looked in the closet and noticed the vacuum cleaner was missing. "Hey," he said to his wife, "I can't find the vacuum. Have you seen it?" The wife looked up from her book. "I got rid of it," she said. "It was just gathering dust."

SEPTEMBER

What smells bad and sounds like a bell?

Dung!

SEPTEMBER

Why should you be wary of a long-term relationship with a tennis player?

Because love means nothing to them.

30
SEPTEMBER

///////////////////////////

Which shrubbery is the most political?

President Bush.

OCTOBER

When I was a boy of fourteen, my father was so ignorant I could hardly stand to have the old man around. But when I got to be twenty-one, I was astonished at how much the old man had learned in seven years.
— attributed to Mark Twain

1
OCTOBER

Parallel lines have so much in common.
It's a bummer they'll never meet.

2
OCTOBER

Did you hear about the restaurant on the moon?

Great food, no atmosphere.

3

OCTOBER

I just found out my toaster isn't waterproof.
I'm shocked.

4

OCTOBER

Two friends walked out of a kitchen supply store.
One friend showed the other that he had stolen
something. "Aren't you afraid of getting caught?"
the friend asked. The thief responded,
"This was just a whisk I was willing to take."

OCTOBER

What did one hat say to the other?

"You stay here. I'll go on ahead."

OCTOBER

My partner left me because of my obsession
with astrology. I should have seen the signs.

OCTOBER

Why is a room full of married people still considered empty?

There isn't a single person in it.

OCTOBER

A pizza walks into a bar and orders a beer. The bartender says, "Sorry, we don't serve food here."

OCTOBER

What do you call a faux noodle?

An impasta.

OCTOBER

What did one continental plate say to the other?

"Between you and me, I think that
earthquake was our fault."

11
OCTOBER

Dad: I don't trust atoms.
Daughter: Why?
Dad: They make everything up.

12
OCTOBER

What lies at the bottom of the ocean and worries?

A nervous wreck.

OCTOBER

If at first you don't succeed, skydiving is probably not for you.

OCTOBER

What did the grape do when he got stepped on?

He let out a little wine.

OCTOBER

How much money does a pirate pay for corn?

A buccaneer.

OCTOBER

A three-legged dog staggered into a saloon and took a seat. The bartender asked, "What brings you to town?" The three-legged dog looked up and in a gruff voice replied, "I'm looking for the man who shot my paw."

OCTOBER

Where did the United States get Alabama, Alaska, Arizona, and Arkansas?

An "A" state sale.

OCTOBER

If pigs could fly, nobody would be eating chicken wings.

OCTOBER

A photo was put on trial for loitering on the wall. "You don't understand!" the photo pleaded. "I was framed!"

OCTOBER

Why was the stick of gum bent out of shape?

It had just been chewed out.

OCTOBER

Did you hear about the coin factory machine that stopped working?

It doesn't make any cents.

OCTOBER

I really like ham, but it'd be a shame if you put an "S" in front and an "E" behind it.

OCTOBER

Why did the desk have to do laundry?

It only had dirty drawers.

OCTOBER

Two old spuds were deeply in love. "You are my sweet potato," one said. "Yes, I yam," the other replied.

25
OCTOBER

I'm so lazy my favorite exercise is the
diddly squat.

26
OCTOBER

What do you call seagulls who fly over the bay?
Bagels.

27
OCTOBER

Knock! Knock!
Who's there?
Felix.
Felix who?
Felixhausted, let me in!

28
OCTOBER

Egg salad is just chicken salad made by
someone with no patience.

OCTOBER

The best way to watch a fishing tournament is live stream.

OCTOBER

Why did the witches have to call a plumber?

Double, double, toilet trouble.

31
OCTOBER

Why don't skeletons ever go trick-or-treating?

Because they have no body to go with.

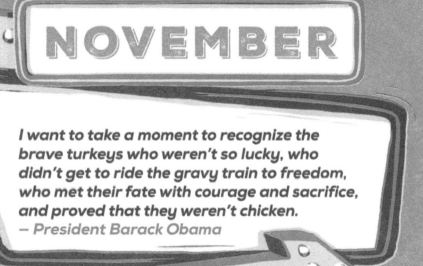

NOVEMBER

I want to take a moment to recognize the brave turkeys who weren't so lucky, who didn't get to ride the gravy train to freedom, who met their fate with courage and sacrifice, and proved that they weren't chicken.
— President Barack Obama

1
NOVEMBER

What's the leading cause of dry skin?
Towels.

2
NOVEMBER

Murphy's Law says that anything that can go wrong, will go wrong. Cole's Law is thinly sliced cabbage with a lot of mayonnaise.

NOVEMBER

A father and a son were on a road trip when they saw a whole field of livestock. The dad pointed out the window and said, "Oh look, a flock of cows!" The son shook his head. "Herd of cows," he corrected his father. "Herd of cows?" the dad said. "Of course I've heard of cows. There's a whole flock of them right there!"

NOVEMBER

Statistically speaking, six out of seven dwarfs aren't happy.

NOVEMBER

If you have 10 apples in one hand and 14 oranges in the other, what do you have?

Really, really big hands.

NOVEMBER

My wife said, "You weren't even listening, were you?" And I thought, that's a pretty weird way to start a conversation.

NOVEMBER

Why are pediatricians always so frustrated?

They have little patients.

NOVEMBER

Adulthood is like losing your parents in the grocery store for the rest of your life.

NOVEMBER

Son: Dad, have you seen my sunglasses?

Dad: No, have you seen my dadglasses?

NOVEMBER

A dad told his daughter not to get too excited about turning 32, since her birthday party would be so short. "Why would it be short?" the daughter asked. The dad grinned and said, "Because it's your 30-second birthday."

11
NOVEMBER

You can tell the difference between an alligator and a crocodile by paying attention to whether the animal will see you later or after a while.

12
NOVEMBER

What do you call a dinosaur with an extensive vocabulary?

A thesaurus.

NOVEMBER

If you jump out of an airplane and your parachute doesn't deploy, you have the rest of your life to fix it.

NOVEMBER

What did one crooked tooth say to the other?

"Brace yourself!"

NOVEMBER

With the rise of self-driving vehicles, eventually there will be a country song about how your truck left you, too.

NOVEMBER

If you use your memory foam pillow in a pillow fight, that's a fight you'll never forget.

NOVEMBER

What do you call a memory of a fart?

Past gas.

NOVEMBER

Two goldfish are in a tank. One says to the other, "Do you know how to drive this thing?"

NOVEMBER

I can cut wood by just looking at it. It's true,
I saw it with my own eyes.

NOVEMBER

**Why couldn't the keyboard get a hat
out of its closet?**

The CAPS LOCK was on.

21

NOVEMBER

If I had a dollar for every time I got suspicious,
I'd wonder who was paying me, and why.

22

NOVEMBER

Why couldn't the fisherman work out anymore?

He pulled a mussel.

NOVEMBER

A guy walked into a bar ... and said, "Ouch!"

NOVEMBER

As a parent, I'm like a cop. Whenever my kids
fight against taking a nap, I tell them they're
going to get more nap time added
on for resisting a rest.

25
NOVEMBER

Have you heard about the new trend of corduroy pillows?

They're making headlines.

26
NOVEMBER

What smells the best at a Thanksgiving dinner?

Typically, it's your nose.

27

NOVEMBER

///

My family asked me to stop making jokes
about the Thanksgiving leftovers,
but I couldn't quit cold turkey.

NOVEMBER

Did you hear about the cheese factory that was demolished?

Nothing left but de Brie.

NOVEMBER

I didn't want to believe that my father was stealing from his road construction job, but when I got home all the signs were all there.

30

NOVEMBER

I love to stargaze, but whenever I do, I can't help but think Orion's Belt is a huge waist of space.

DECEMBER

Adults are just outdated children. — Dr. Seuss

1
DECEMBER

What is a pigeon's favorite type of poem?
A hai coo-coo.

2
DECEMBER

Two buckets were hanging out. One bucket said to the other, "Are you feeling sick?" The other replied, "No, why?" The first bucket said, "You're a little pail."

DECEMBER

What do you call a snowman with a six pack?

The Abdominal Snowman.

DECEMBER

Did you see the snowman at the farmers' market looking at carrots?

He was picking his nose.

DECEMBER

As I handed my dad his 70th birthday card, he looked at me with tears in his eyes and said, "You know, one would have been enough."

DECEMBER

What do your dog and your phone have in common?

They both have collar ID.

DECEMBER

Why did the old man fall in a deep, narrow pool of water?

He couldn't see that well.

DECEMBER

A buttload of underwear is exactly one pair.

DECEMBER

If a cannibal shakes your hand,
he considers you finger food.

DECEMBER

Son: Will you hand me my bookmark?

Dad: I know my name is Mark, but
please call me "Dad."

DECEMBER

What do you call a criminal who's being a jerk while he's walking down a flight of stairs?

A condescending con, descending.

DECEMBER

As a scarecrow, I know my job isn't right for everyone. But hay, it's in my jeans.

DECEMBER

I have an irrational fear of elevators and I'll be taking steps to avoid them.

14
DECEMBER

The Queen of England flew to the United States for a big meeting. Her plane landed early, so she asked her driver if she could take the car for a spin—she had never driven in America and wanted to give it a try. She was weaving in and out of her lane when suddenly a siren blared and a cop pulled her over. As soon as he saw the queen, his eyes went wide, and he told her to hold tight. He ran back to his car radio. "Sheriff, I have a situation!" he exclaimed. "I pulled over someone very important." "Is it the governor?" asked the sheriff. "No, sir, bigger," the cop responded. "A movie star?" "No, sir, more important." "Well, who is it?" asked the sheriff. "Honestly," said the cop, "I'm not sure, but the Queen of England is his driver!"

DECEMBER

I tried a page out of a vegan recipe book last night,
and honestly, it tasted like paper.

DECEMBER

Why did the waiter put a book under a table leg?

The customer ordered a lean steak.

17

DECEMBER

Two muffins were sitting in an oven. The first muffin turned to the second and said, "Boy, it sure is hot in here." And the second muffin thought, "WOOO!! A TALKING MUFFIN!!!"

18

DECEMBER

Nurse: Doctor, there's a patient who says he's invisible.
Doctor: Well, tell him I can't see him right now.

19
DECEMBER

What do you do when you see a spaceman?

Park your car, man.

20
DECEMBER

Why do melons have weddings?

They cantaloupe.

DECEMBER

Why was the broom late for work?

She swept in.

DECEMBER

If you're looking for a wise investment,
buy a barn. It's a stable business.

23
DECEMBER

What do you call a group of whales playing killer music?

An orcastra.

24
DECEMBER

A sunburnt man named Rudolph looked out the window, turned to his wife, and said, "It's going to rain." "How do you know?" she asked. "Because Rudolph the Red knows rain, dear."

25
DECEMBER

I've got a friend who is obsessed with Santa's helpers. He's so elf-centered.

26

DECEMBER

A man balanced on the shoulders of a couple of vampires was caught stealing in a supermarket. He was charged with shoplifting on two counts.

DECEMBER

When you have a bladder infection,
urine trouble.

DECEMBER

How does the moon cut his hair?

Eclipse it.

DECEMBER

I'm deathly allergic to bears. One bite, and it's straight to the emergency room for me.

DECEMBER

I'm a big fan of nostalgia, but it's not what it used to be.

31
DECEMBER

//////////////////////////////

What did the director say at the end of her film about gyros?

"That's a wrap, people."

ACKNOWLEDGMENTS

Mark Harmon, Larry Calmus, Zach Calmus, Andy Stangohr and, of course, our wives and kids for listening to us test out these jokes for hours on end.

TAYLOR CALMUS

(also known as "Dude Dad") is an actor/comedian, husband, father of two, and the creator of the popular Internet video series *Dude Dad*. The series showcases everything from his comedic take on fatherhood to his over-the-top dad inventions, and it has become a viral hit with millions of viewers.

FOLLOW TAYLOR

@DudeDad on Facebook & YouTube | @DudeDadVlog on Instagram & Twitter

www.DudeDad.com

PETER L. HARMON

is a husband, a pug lover, and a dad to two sons. He's the
author of *the* YA book series The Happenstances; he is also
an independent screenwriter, a television producer, and a
frequent collaborator with Taylor.

FOLLOW PETER

@PeterLHarmon on Instagram and Twitter

www.PeterLHarmon.com

9 781641 526555